THIS COCKTAIL RECIPE BOOK BELONGS TO:

MY AWESOME COCKTAIL RECIPES

RECIPE

PAGE

MY AWESOME COCKTAIL RECIPES

RECIPE

MY AWESOME COCKTAIL RECIPES

RECIPE	PAGE

MY AWESOME COCKTAIL RECIPES

RECIPE

PAGE

MEASUREMENT CONVERSION CHART

CUPS, SPOONS & LIQUIDS

MEASURE	OUNCES	EQUIVALENTS	LITERS
1/4 tsp			1 ml
1/2 tsp			2.5 ml
1 tsp		1/3 Tbsp	5 ml
2 tsp	1/3 fl oz	2/3 Tbsp	10 ml
1 Tbsp	1/2 fl oz	3 tsp	15 ml
2 Tbsp	1 fl oz	1/8 cup (6 tsp)	30 ml
1/4 cup	2 fl oz	4 Tbsp	60 ml
1/3 cup	2 2/3 fl oz	5 Tbsp & 1 tsp	80 ml
1/2 cup	4 fl oz	8 Tbsp	120 ml
2/3 cup	5 1/3 fl oz	10 Tbsp & 2 tsp	160 ml
3/4 cup	6 fl oz	12 Tbsp	180 ml
7/8 cup	7 fl oz	14 Tbsp	200 ml
1 cup (1/2 pint)	8 fl oz	16 Tbsp	220 ml
2 cups (1 pint)	16 fl oz	32 Tbsp	250 ml
1 quart	32 fl oz	4 cups	950 ml
1 quart plus 1/4 cup	34 fl oz	4 cups & 4 Tbsp	1 L
1 gallon (4 quarts)	128 fl oz	16 cups	3.8 L

WEIGHT

OUNCES	POUNDS	GRAMS
1/4 ounce		7 g
1/2 ounce		15 g
3/4 ounce		21 g
1 ounce		28 g
2 ounces		57 g
3 ounces		85 g
4 ounces	1/4 pound	113 g
8 ounces	1/2 pound	227 g
16 ounces	1 pound	454 g
35.2 ounces	2.2 pounds	1 kg

TEMPERATURE

FAHRENHEIT	CELSIUS
250° F	120° C
275° F	140° C
300° F	150° C
325° F	160° C
350° F	180° C
375° F	190° C
400° F	200° C
425° F	220° C
450° F	230° C
475° F	245° C

COCKTAIL

DATE .... **DIFFICULTY** ○ ○ ○ ○ ○ **RATING** ☆ ☆ ☆ ☆ ☆

INGREDIENTS

....
....
....
....
....
....
....
....
....
....
....
....
....

DIRECTIONS

....
....
....
....
....
....
....
....
....
....
....
....
....
....

GLASS

GARNISH ....
....
....

NOTES ....
....
....
....

COCKTAIL

01 DATE .... DIFFICULTY ○○○○○ RATING ☆☆☆☆☆

INGREDIENTS

DIRECTIONS

GLASS

GARNISH

NOTES

8

COCKTAIL

DATE _____ DIFFICULTY ○○○○○ RATING ☆☆☆☆☆

INGREDIENTS

DIRECTIONS

GLASS

GARNISH

NOTES

9

COCKTAIL

DATE _____ DIFFICULTY ○○○○○ RATING ☆☆☆☆☆

INGREDIENTS

DIRECTIONS

GLASS

GARNISH

NOTES

COCKTAIL _____

📅 **01** DATE _____   DIFFICULTY ○ ○ ○ ○ ○   RATING ☆ ☆ ☆ ☆ ☆

INGREDIENTS

_____
_____
_____
_____
_____
_____
_____
_____
_____
_____
_____
_____
_____

DIRECTIONS

_____
_____
_____
_____
_____
_____
_____
_____
_____
_____
_____
_____
_____
_____

GLASS

GARNISH _____
_____
_____
_____

NOTES _____
_____
_____
_____
_____

COCKTAIL

📅 DATE .... DIFFICULTY ○ ○ ○ ○ ○ RATING ☆ ☆ ☆ ☆ ☆

INGREDIENTS

DIRECTIONS

🍷 GLASS

💐 GARNISH

📝 NOTES

COCKTAIL ....

📅 01 DATE ....   **DIFFICULTY** ○ ○ ○ ○ ○   **RATING** ☆ ☆ ☆ ☆ ☆

INGREDIENTS

DIRECTIONS

🍷 GLASS

🌿 GARNISH ....

📓 NOTES ....

COCKTAIL

01 DATE _____   **DIFFICULTY** ○ ○ ○ ○ ○   **RATING** ☆ ☆ ☆ ☆ ☆

INGREDIENTS

DIRECTIONS

GLASS

GARNISH

NOTES

COCKTAIL

01 DATE .... DIFFICULTY ○ ○ ○ ○ ○   RATING ☆ ☆ ☆ ☆ ☆

INGREDIENTS

DIRECTIONS

GLASS

GARNISH

NOTES

COCKTAIL

📅 DATE .... DIFFICULTY ○○○○○ RATING ☆☆☆☆☆

INGREDIENTS

DIRECTIONS

GLASS

GARNISH

NOTES

COCKTAIL

DIFFICULTY ○ ○ ○ ○ ○   RATING ☆ ☆ ☆ ☆ ☆

INGREDIENTS

DIRECTIONS

GLASS

GARNISH

NOTES

COCKTAIL

01 DATE .... DIFFICULTY ○ ○ ○ ○ ○   RATING ☆ ☆ ☆ ☆ ☆

INGREDIENTS

DIRECTIONS

GLASS

GARNISH

NOTES

COCKTAIL

📅 DATE .... DIFFICULTY ○○○○○ RATING ☆☆☆☆☆

INGREDIENTS

DIRECTIONS

🥂 GLASS

🌿 GARNISH

📝 NOTES

COCKTAIL

01 DATE _____   DIFFICULTY ○ ○ ○ ○ ○   RATING ☆ ☆ ☆ ☆ ☆

INGREDIENTS

DIRECTIONS

GLASS

GARNISH _____

NOTES _____

COCKTAIL

....

📅 **DATE** .... **DIFFICULTY** ○ ○ ○ ○ ○ **RATING** ☆ ☆ ☆ ☆ ☆

🍾 **INGREDIENTS**

....
....
....
....
....
....
....
....
....
....
....
....
....

🍸 **DIRECTIONS**

....
....
....
....
....
....
....
....
....
....
....
....
....

🥂 **GLASS**

🍹 **GARNISH** ....
....
....

📝 **NOTES** ....
....
....
....
....

COCKTAIL _____

📅 **01** DATE _____   DIFFICULTY ○○○○○   RATING ☆☆☆☆☆

🍾 **INGREDIENTS**

_____
_____
_____
_____
_____
_____
_____
_____
_____
_____
_____
_____

🍸 **DIRECTIONS**

_____
_____
_____
_____
_____
_____
_____
_____
_____
_____
_____
_____
_____
_____
_____

🍷 **GLASS**

🌿 **GARNISH** _____
_____
_____
_____

📝 **NOTES** _____
_____
_____
_____
_____

COCKTAIL

DATE .... **DIFFICULTY** ○ ○ ○ ○ ○ **RATING** ☆ ☆ ☆ ☆ ☆

INGREDIENTS

DIRECTIONS

GLASS

GARNISH

NOTES

COCKTAIL

DATE .... DIFFICULTY ○ ○ ○ ○ ○ RATING ☆ ☆ ☆ ☆ ☆

INGREDIENTS

DIRECTIONS

GLASS

GARNISH

NOTES

COCKTAIL ....

INGREDIENTS

....
....
....
....
....
....
....
....
....
....
....
....
....

DIRECTIONS

....
....
....
....
....
....
....
....
....
....
....
....
....
....
....

GLASS

GARNISH
....
....
....

NOTES
....
....
....
....
....

COCKTAIL

01 DATE _____   DIFFICULTY ○ ○ ○ ○ ○   RATING ☆ ☆ ☆ ☆ ☆

INGREDIENTS

DIRECTIONS

GLASS

GARNISH

NOTES

COCTAIL

01 DATE _____   DIFFICULTY ○○○○○   RATING ☆☆☆☆☆

INGREDIENTS

DIRECTIONS

GLASS

GARNISH

NOTES

COCKTAIL ....

📅 **01** DATE .... DIFFICULTY ○ ○ ○ ○ ○ RATING ☆ ☆ ☆ ☆ ☆

🍾 **INGREDIENTS**

🍸 **DIRECTIONS**

🍷 GLASS

🌿 GARNISH ....
....
....
....

📝 NOTES ....
....
....
....

COCKTAIL

DATE _____   DIFFICULTY ○ ○ ○ ○ ○   RATING ☆ ☆ ☆ ☆ ☆

INGREDIENTS

DIRECTIONS

GLASS

GARNISH

NOTES

COCKTAIL

📅 **01 DATE** .... **DIFFICULTY** ○ ○ ○ ○ ○   **RATING** ☆ ☆ ☆ ☆ ☆

🍾 **INGREDIENTS**

🍸 **DIRECTIONS**

🍷 **GLASS**

🌿 **GARNISH** ....

📝 **NOTES** ....

COCKTAIL ....

📅 **DATE** .... **DIFFICULTY** ○ ○ ○ ○ ○ **RATING** ☆ ☆ ☆ ☆ ☆

🍾 INGREDIENTS

....
....
....
....
....
....
....
....
....
....
....
....

🍸 DIRECTIONS

....
....
....
....
....
....
....
....
....
....
....
....
....

🍷 **GLASS**

🌿 **GARNISH** ....
....
....

📝 **NOTES** ....
....
....
....
....

COCKTAIL

01 DATE _____ **DIFFICULTY** ○ ○ ○ ○ ○ **RATING** ☆ ☆ ☆ ☆ ☆

INGREDIENTS

DIRECTIONS

GLASS

GARNISH

NOTES

COCKTAIL

01 DATE .... DIFFICULTY ○○○○○ RATING ☆☆☆☆☆

INGREDIENTS

....
....
....
....
....
....
....
....
....
....
....
....

DIRECTIONS

....
....
....
....
....
....
....
....
....
....
....
....

GLASS

GARNISH ....
....
....
....

NOTES ....
....
....
....

COCKTAIL

DATE _____ DIFFICULTY ○○○○○ RATING ☆☆☆☆☆

INGREDIENTS

DIRECTIONS

GLASS

GARNISH

NOTES

COCKTAIL

01 DATE .... DIFFICULTY ○ ○ ○ ○ ○ RATING ☆ ☆ ☆ ☆ ☆

INGREDIENTS

DIRECTIONS

GLASS

GARNISH ....

NOTES ....

COCKTAIL

01 DATE _____ DIFFICULTY ○ ○ ○ ○ ○ RATING ☆ ☆ ☆ ☆ ☆

INGREDIENTS

DIRECTIONS

GLASS

GARNISH

NOTES

COCKTAIL ....

📅 **DATE** ....   **DIFFICULTY** ○ ○ ○ ○ ○   **RATING** ☆ ☆ ☆ ☆ ☆

🍾 **INGREDIENTS**

🍸 **DIRECTIONS**

🍷 **GLASS**

🌿 **GARNISH** ....

📄 **NOTES** ....

COCKTAIL

DATE _____   DIFFICULTY ○ ○ ○ ○ ○   RATING ☆ ☆ ☆ ☆ ☆

INGREDIENTS

DIRECTIONS

GLASS

GARNISH _____

NOTES _____

COCKTAIL

📅 **01 DATE** .... **DIFFICULTY** ○○○○○ **RATING** ☆☆☆☆☆

🍾 **INGREDIENTS**

🍸 **DIRECTIONS**

🍷 **GLASS**

🌿 **GARNISH**

📝 **NOTES**

COCKTAIL

DATE _____   DIFFICULTY ○○○○○   RATING ☆☆☆☆☆

INGREDIENTS

DIRECTIONS

GLASS

GARNISH

NOTES

COCKTAIL

DATE .... DIFFICULTY ○ ○ ○ ○ ○ RATING ☆ ☆ ☆ ☆ ☆

INGREDIENTS

DIRECTIONS

GLASS

GARNISH

NOTES

COCKTAIL

DATE .... DIFFICULTY ○○○○○ RATING ☆☆☆☆☆

INGREDIENTS

DIRECTIONS

GLASS

GARNISH

NOTES

COCKTAIL

DATE .... DIFFICULTY ○ ○ ○ ○ ○ RATING ☆ ☆ ☆ ☆ ☆

INGREDIENTS

DIRECTIONS

GLASS

GARNISH

NOTES

COCKTAIL

01 DATE _____   DIFFICULTY ○ ○ ○ ○ ○   RATING ☆ ☆ ☆ ☆ ☆

INGREDIENTS

DIRECTIONS

GLASS

GARNISH

NOTES

COCKTAIL ....

📅 **01** DATE .... **DIFFICULTY** ○ ○ ○ ○ ○   **RATING** ☆ ☆ ☆ ☆ ☆

🍾 **INGREDIENTS**

🍸 **DIRECTIONS**

🍷 **GLASS**

💐 **GARNISH** ....
....
....

📓 **NOTES** ....
....
....
....

COCKTAIL

INGREDIENTS

DIRECTIONS

GLASS

GARNISH

NOTES

COCKTAIL

DATE _____ DIFFICULTY ○ ○ ○ ○ ○ RATING ☆ ☆ ☆ ☆ ☆

INGREDIENTS

DIRECTIONS

GLASS

GARNISH

NOTES

COCKTAIL

DATE _____   DIFFICULTY ○ ○ ○ ○ ○   RATING ☆ ☆ ☆ ☆ ☆

INGREDIENTS

DIRECTIONS

GLASS

GARNISH

NOTES

COCKTAIL

INGREDIENTS

DIRECTIONS

🍷 GLASS

🌿 GARNISH

📝 NOTES

COCKTAIL

01 DATE _____ DIFFICULTY ○ ○ ○ ○ ○ RATING ☆ ☆ ☆ ☆ ☆

INGREDIENTS

DIRECTIONS

GLASS

GARNISH

NOTES

COCKTAIL

DATE .... DIFFICULTY ○○○○○ RATING ☆☆☆☆☆

INGREDIENTS

DIRECTIONS

GLASS

GARNISH ....
....
....

NOTES ....
....
....
....

COCKTAIL

DATE _____   DIFFICULTY ○ ○ ○ ○ ○   RATING ☆ ☆ ☆ ☆ ☆

INGREDIENTS

DIRECTIONS

GLASS

GARNISH

NOTES

COCKTAIL ....

01 DATE ....   DIFFICULTY ○ ○ ○ ○ ○   RATING ☆ ☆ ☆ ☆ ☆

INGREDIENTS

DIRECTIONS

GLASS

GARNISH ....
....
....
....

NOTES ....
....
....
....
....

COCKTAIL

DATE .... DIFFICULTY ○○○○○ RATING ☆☆☆☆☆

INGREDIENTS

DIRECTIONS

GLASS

GARNISH

NOTES

54

COCKTAIL

DATE .... DIFFICULTY ○ ○ ○ ○ ○ RATING ☆ ☆ ☆ ☆ ☆

INGREDIENTS

DIRECTIONS

GLASS

GARNISH

NOTES

COCKTAIL

INGREDIENTS

DIRECTIONS

GLASS

GARNISH

NOTES

COCKTAIL

01 DATE _____ DIFFICULTY ○ ○ ○ ○ ○ RATING ☆ ☆ ☆ ☆ ☆

INGREDIENTS

_____ _____
_____ _____
_____ _____
_____ _____
_____ _____
_____ _____
_____ _____
_____ _____
_____ _____
_____ _____
_____ _____
_____ _____

DIRECTIONS

_____
_____
_____
_____
_____
_____
_____
_____
_____
_____
_____
_____
_____

GLASS

GARNISH _____
_____
_____

NOTES _____
_____
_____
_____

COCKTAIL

INGREDIENTS

DIRECTIONS

GLASS

GARNISH

NOTES

COCKTAIL

01 DATE ....

DIFFICULTY ○ ○ ○ ○ ○

RATING ☆ ☆ ☆ ☆ ☆

INGREDIENTS

DIRECTIONS

GLASS

GARNISH ....

NOTES ....

COCKTAIL

01 DATE _____   DIFFICULTY ○ ○ ○ ○ ○   RATING ☆ ☆ ☆ ☆ ☆

INGREDIENTS

DIRECTIONS

GLASS

GARNISH

NOTES

COCKTAIL ....

01 DATE .... DIFFICULTY ○ ○ ○ ○ ○   RATING ☆ ☆ ☆ ☆ ☆

INGREDIENTS

DIRECTIONS

GLASS

GARNISH

NOTES

COCKTAIL

01 DATE .... DIFFICULTY ○ ○ ○ ○ ○ RATING ☆ ☆ ☆ ☆ ☆

INGREDIENTS

DIRECTIONS

GLASS

GARNISH

NOTES

COCKTAIL

01 DATE _____   DIFFICULTY ○ ○ ○ ○ ○   RATING ☆ ☆ ☆ ☆ ☆

INGREDIENTS

DIRECTIONS

GLASS

GARNISH

NOTES

COCKTAIL

DATE .... DIFFICULTY ○ ○ ○ ○ ○   RATING ☆ ☆ ☆ ☆ ☆

INGREDIENTS

DIRECTIONS

GLASS

GARNISH

NOTES

COCKTAIL

DATE _____   DIFFICULTY ○ ○ ○ ○ ○   RATING ☆ ☆ ☆ ☆ ☆

INGREDIENTS

DIRECTIONS

GLASS

GARNISH

NOTES

COCKTAIL

DATE _____ **DIFFICULTY** ○ ○ ○ ○ ○ **RATING** ☆ ☆ ☆ ☆ ☆

INGREDIENTS

DIRECTIONS

GLASS

GARNISH

NOTES

66

COCKTAIL ....

INGREDIENTS

....
....
....
....
....
....
....
....
....
....
....
....
....

DIRECTIONS

....
....
....
....
....
....
....
....
....
....
....
....
....
....
....
....
....

🍷 GLASS

🌿 GARNISH ....
....
....
....

📝 NOTES ....
....
....
....
....

COCKTAIL

01 DATE .... DIFFICULTY ○○○○○ RATING ☆☆☆☆☆

INGREDIENTS

DIRECTIONS

GLASS

GARNISH

NOTES

COCKTAIL

INGREDIENTS

DIRECTIONS

GLASS

GARNISH

NOTES

COCKTAIL

01 DATE _____   **DIFFICULTY** ○○○○○   **RATING** ☆☆☆☆☆

INGREDIENTS

DIRECTIONS

GLASS

GARNISH _____

NOTES _____

COCKTAIL

DATE _____   DIFFICULTY ○○○○○   RATING ☆☆☆☆☆

INGREDIENTS

DIRECTIONS

GLASS

GARNISH

NOTES

COCKTAIL

01 DATE .... DIFFICULTY ○○○○○ RATING ☆☆☆☆☆

INGREDIENTS

DIRECTIONS

GLASS

GARNISH ....

NOTES ....

COCKTAIL

01 DATE .... DIFFICULTY ○ ○ ○ ○ ○ RATING ☆ ☆ ☆ ☆ ☆

INGREDIENTS

DIRECTIONS

GLASS

GARNISH

NOTES

COCKTAIL

01 DATE .... DIFFICULTY ○ ○ ○ ○ ○ RATING ☆ ☆ ☆ ☆ ☆

INGREDIENTS

DIRECTIONS

GLASS

GARNISH

NOTES

COCKTAIL

DATE .... DIFFICULTY ○ ○ ○ ○ ○   RATING ☆ ☆ ☆ ☆ ☆

INGREDIENTS

DIRECTIONS

GLASS

GARNISH

NOTES

COCKTAIL _____

INGREDIENTS

DIRECTIONS

GLASS

GARNISH _____

NOTES _____

COCKTAIL

DATE .... DIFFICULTY ○ ○ ○ ○ ○ RATING ☆ ☆ ☆ ☆ ☆

INGREDIENTS

DIRECTIONS

GLASS

GARNISH

NOTES

77

COCKTAIL

01 DATE .... DIFFICULTY ○○○○○ RATING ☆☆☆☆☆

INGREDIENTS

DIRECTIONS

GLASS

GARNISH ....

NOTES ....

COCTAIL

📅 DATE .... DIFFICULTY ○ ○ ○ ○ ○ RATING ☆ ☆ ☆ ☆ ☆

INGREDIENTS

DIRECTIONS

🍷 GLASS

💐 GARNISH

📓 NOTES

COCKTAIL

DATE .... **DIFFICULTY** ○ ○ ○ ○ ○ **RATING** ☆ ☆ ☆ ☆ ☆

INGREDIENTS

DIRECTIONS

GLASS

GARNISH ....

NOTES ....

COCKTAIL ....

📅 **01** DATE ....   DIFFICULTY ○○○○○   RATING ☆☆☆☆☆

🍾 INGREDIENTS

....
....
....
....
....
....
....
....
....
....
....
....

🍸 DIRECTIONS

....
....
....
....
....
....
....
....
....
....
....
....
....
....

🍷 GLASS

🌿 GARNISH ....
....
....
....

📝 NOTES ....
....
....
....

COCKTAIL

INGREDIENTS

DIRECTIONS

GLASS

GARNISH

NOTES

COCKTAIL _____

📅 **01** DATE _____   DIFFICULTY ○ ○ ○ ○ ○   RATING ☆ ☆ ☆ ☆ ☆

INGREDIENTS

_____
_____
_____
_____
_____
_____
_____
_____
_____
_____
_____
_____
_____

DIRECTIONS

_____
_____
_____
_____
_____
_____
_____
_____
_____
_____
_____
_____
_____
_____

🍷 GLASS

🍹 GARNISH _____
_____
_____

📝 NOTES _____
_____
_____
_____
_____

COCKTAIL _____

01 DATE _____   **DIFFICULTY** ○○○○○   **RATING** ☆☆☆☆☆

INGREDIENTS

_____
_____
_____
_____
_____
_____
_____
_____
_____
_____
_____
_____
_____

DIRECTIONS

_____
_____
_____
_____
_____
_____
_____
_____
_____
_____
_____
_____
_____
_____

GLASS

GARNISH _____
_____
_____

NOTES _____
_____
_____
_____

COCKTAIL

![01] DATE .... DIFFICULTY ○ ○ ○ ○ ○ RATING ☆ ☆ ☆ ☆ ☆

INGREDIENTS

DIRECTIONS

GLASS

GARNISH

NOTES

COCKTAIL

DATE .... DIFFICULTY ○ ○ ○ ○ ○ RATING ☆ ☆ ☆ ☆ ☆

INGREDIENTS

DIRECTIONS

GLASS

GARNISH

NOTES

COCKTAIL

INGREDIENTS

DIRECTIONS

GLASS

GARNISH

NOTES

COCKTAIL

📅 **01** DATE _____ DIFFICULTY ○ ○ ○ ○ ○ RATING ☆ ☆ ☆ ☆ ☆

🍾 **INGREDIENTS**

🍸 **DIRECTIONS**

🍷 **GLASS**

🌿 **GARNISH**

📝 **NOTES**

COCKTAIL

_____

📅 **01** DATE _____ DIFFICULTY ⃝ ⃝ ⃝ ⃝ ⃝   RATING ☆ ☆ ☆ ☆ ☆

🍾 **INGREDIENTS**

_____
_____
_____
_____
_____
_____
_____
_____
_____
_____
_____

🍸 **DIRECTIONS**

_____
_____
_____
_____
_____
_____
_____
_____
_____
_____
_____
_____
_____

🍷 **GLASS**

🌿 **GARNISH** _____
_____
_____
_____

📝 **NOTES** _____
_____
_____
_____

COCKTAIL ....

01 DATE .... **DIFFICULTY** ○ ○ ○ ○ ○ **RATING** ☆ ☆ ☆ ☆ ☆

INGREDIENTS

DIRECTIONS

GLASS

GARNISH ....
....
....

NOTES ....
....
....
....
....

COCKTAIL ....

01 DATE ....   DIFFICULTY ○ ○ ○ ○ ○   RATING ☆ ☆ ☆ ☆ ☆

INGREDIENTS

DIRECTIONS

GLASS

GARNISH

NOTES

COCKTAIL

01 DATE _____ **DIFFICULTY** ○ ○ ○ ○ ○ **RATING** ☆ ☆ ☆ ☆ ☆

INGREDIENTS

DIRECTIONS

GLASS

GARNISH

NOTES

COCKTAIL

DATE .... DIFFICULTY ○ ○ ○ ○ ○ RATING ☆ ☆ ☆ ☆ ☆

INGREDIENTS

DIRECTIONS

GLASS

GARNISH

NOTES

COCKTAIL

DATE .... DIFFICULTY ○ ○ ○ ○ ○ RATING ☆ ☆ ☆ ☆ ☆

INGREDIENTS

DIRECTIONS

GLASS

GARNISH

NOTES

COCKTAIL

INGREDIENTS

DIRECTIONS

GLASS

GARNISH

NOTES

COCKTAIL

01 DATE _____   **DIFFICULTY** ○ ○ ○ ○ ○   **RATING** ☆ ☆ ☆ ☆ ☆

INGREDIENTS

DIRECTIONS

GLASS

GARNISH

NOTES

COCKTAIL ....

INGREDIENTS

....
....
....
....
....
....
....
....
....
....
....

DIRECTIONS

....
....
....
....
....
....
....
....
....
....
....
....

GLASS

GARNISH
....
....
....

NOTES ....
....
....
....

97

COCKTAIL

01 DATE _____   DIFFICULTY ○ ○ ○ ○ ○   RATING ☆ ☆ ☆ ☆ ☆

INGREDIENTS

DIRECTIONS

GLASS

GARNISH

NOTES

COCKTAIL

01 DATE .... **DIFFICULTY** ○ ○ ○ ○ ○ **RATING** ☆ ☆ ☆ ☆ ☆

INGREDIENTS

DIRECTIONS

GLASS

GARNISH

NOTES

COCKTAIL ....

DATE .... DIFFICULTY ○ ○ ○ ○ ○ RATING ☆ ☆ ☆ ☆ ☆

INGREDIENTS

DIRECTIONS

GLASS

GARNISH ....

NOTES ....

100

COCKTAIL

01 DATE _____   DIFFICULTY ○ ○ ○ ○ ○   RATING ☆ ☆ ☆ ☆ ☆

INGREDIENTS

DIRECTIONS

GLASS

GARNISH

NOTES

COCKTAIL

DATE _____   DIFFICULTY ○ ○ ○ ○ ○   RATING ☆ ☆ ☆ ☆ ☆

INGREDIENTS

DIRECTIONS

GLASS

GARNISH

NOTES

COCKTAIL

DATE .... DIFFICULTY ○○○○○ RATING ☆☆☆☆☆

INGREDIENTS

DIRECTIONS

GLASS

GARNISH ....

NOTES ....

COCKTAIL

DATE _____   DIFFICULTY ○○○○○   RATING ☆☆☆☆☆

INGREDIENTS

DIRECTIONS

GLASS

GARNISH _____

NOTES _____

COCTAIL

DATE .... DIFFICULTY ○ ○ ○ ○ ○   RATING ☆ ☆ ☆ ☆ ☆

INGREDIENTS

DIRECTIONS

GLASS

GARNISH

NOTES

COCKTAIL

DATE _____ DIFFICULTY ○○○○○ RATING ☆☆☆☆☆

INGREDIENTS

DIRECTIONS

GLASS

GARNISH

NOTES

COCKTAIL

INGREDIENTS

DIRECTIONS

GLASS

GARNISH

NOTES

COCKTAIL

INGREDIENTS

DIRECTIONS

GLASS

GARNISH

NOTES

COCKTAIL ....

01 DATE ....   **DIFFICULTY** ⭘⭘⭘⭘⭘   **RATING** ☆☆☆☆☆

INGREDIENTS

....
....
....
....
....
....
....
....
....
....
....

DIRECTIONS

....
....
....
....
....
....
....
....
....
....
....
....
....
....

GLASS

GARNISH ....
....
....

NOTES ....
....
....
....

COCKTAIL

DATE .... **DIFFICULTY** ⭘⭘⭘⭘⭘ **RATING** ☆☆☆☆☆

INGREDIENTS

DIRECTIONS

GLASS

GARNISH

NOTES

COCKTAIL

INGREDIENTS

DIRECTIONS

GLASS

GARNISH

NOTES

COCKTAIL

DATE _____

DIFFICULTY ○ ○ ○ ○ ○

RATING ☆ ☆ ☆ ☆ ☆

INGREDIENTS

DIRECTIONS

GLASS

GARNISH

NOTES

COCKTAIL

DATE _____ DIFFICULTY ○ ○ ○ ○ ○ RATING ☆ ☆ ☆ ☆ ☆

INGREDIENTS

DIRECTIONS

GLASS

GARNISH _____

NOTES _____

COCKTAIL

INGREDIENTS

DIRECTIONS

GLASS

GARNISH

NOTES

COCKTAIL

DATE .... **DIFFICULTY** ○ ○ ○ ○ ○ **RATING** ☆ ☆ ☆ ☆ ☆

INGREDIENTS

DIRECTIONS

GLASS

GARNISH

NOTES

COCKTAIL

DATE _____   DIFFICULTY ○ ○ ○ ○ ○   RATING ☆ ☆ ☆ ☆ ☆

INGREDIENTS

DIRECTIONS

GLASS

GARNISH

NOTES

COCKTAIL

01 DATE .... DIFFICULTY ○○○○○ RATING ☆☆☆☆☆

INGREDIENTS

DIRECTIONS

GLASS

GARNISH

NOTES

COCKTAIL

DATE ....

DIFFICULTY ○ ○ ○ ○ ○

RATING ☆ ☆ ☆ ☆ ☆

INGREDIENTS

DIRECTIONS

GLASS

GARNISH

NOTES

COCKTAIL

DATE ....

DIFFICULTY ○ ○ ○ ○ ○

RATING ☆ ☆ ☆ ☆ ☆

INGREDIENTS

DIRECTIONS

GLASS

GARNISH

NOTES

Contact:

Gerald Curk Marketing & Design
Waldschmidtstraße 9 • 93051 Regensburg
GERMANY

Any questions or suggestions: servus@curk.de

Made in the USA
Monee, IL
01 December 2020